How I Made $40,000 Working Part-Time
And You Can Too!

To order additional copies, please contact us.
BookSurge, LLC
www.booksurge.com
1-866-308-6235
orders@booksurge.com

How I Made $40,000 Working Part-Time
And You Can Too!

Chad Burns

2006

How I Made $40,000 Working Part-Time

Part-Time
And You Can Too!

Index

Introduction

What I am about to show you is one of the easiest businesses to get into and one of the cheapest businesses to start up. I understand you don't have tens of thousands of dollars to spend in starting a business. What average hard working person does? I know I didn't. That's why I want to show you how to do this without spending a bunch of money! I want to be able to help the average working man or woman to get those little extras in life. I was shown how to do it and I started up for less than $900 before we got our first client. My wife and I now own a business that does over $100,000 annually!! We have five employees and are still growing and we've only been in business for over 6 years!! Now don't worry if you don't have the $900.00 to start with because I will show you how to do this a little at a time. This isn't hard to do. It just takes a little bit of time.

Now let me tell you my story!

I was a cop who had become very tired of working 10-12 hour days five days a week and then spending my days off in court or waiting around to go to court. I had become very disenfranchised with my job. I had basically gotten to where I hated to go to work! I was tired of working all the time and feeling like I wasn't getting anywhere. Sound familiar? My wife and I both were cops and we were both looking for "something better". Well, a lot of people will tell you that anything else is something better. When you work for yourself, it IS better!! The advantages are:

- You work for yourself.
- You work as much as you need to or want to.
- You work when you want to

- You don't have to put up with favoritism or office politics
  - YOU CAN MAKE AS MUCH $$$$ AS YOU WANT!!

Yes I must admit, that last one did appeal to me. I just wanted nice things for my family and me. I wanted my daughter to have nice things and for my wife to drive a nice car and for us to spend time on vacations as a family! Is that so terrible? I don't think so. I was tired of trying to help people who didn't want my help and working in a job that was high in stress, suicide and alcoholism! Doesn't sound like much fun huh?

Ok, well now we come to the good stuff. My wife and I both liked business and wanted very much to start our own. So we looked at various ideas. We also spent a lot of time and money on the so-called "get rich quick" schemes from the real estate deals to placing ads to the Internet businesses to whatever!! WE TRIED IT ALL!! All of them promised so much and delivered so little. I did one business exactly how they told me to do it and STILL nothing happened!!

So it was time to do it on our own. We didn't have the big money to invest in a franchise and we needed something cheap and easy to start. So we looked at (drum roll) Office Cleaning! I had worked for a few years as a janitor for a school when I was younger so I had an idea of what it took. Also keep in mind, this is not DEEP CLEANING. This is LIGHT CLEANING! (Sweeping, mopping, vacuuming, dumping trash and cleaning bathrooms.) Everyone can do that! And businesses will pay you very well to do it for them! Some folks do it on the side for vacations or new cars and others do it as a full on business like myself.

Why am I telling you about this? Because there is so much business out there I couldn't possibly do it all myself. Take a look at the yellow pages! THERE IS YOUR CLIENT LIST!! YOU CAN DO THIS BUSINESS ANYWHERE!

Now there are franchises out there that you can join for $10-$25,000 and you will be in business immediately! But you will pay royalty fees, start-up costs, investing in equipment and inventory, etc. and it gets expensive FAST!

This is not a "get rich quick" scheme. This is a legitimate business opportunity. I know one lady who was selling the secrets to her cleaning business for over $300!! I know because I bought her marketing part of it for my business!

I will show you how to be up and running for less than $900.00. To be legitimate and have a real business, you will end up spending around that. Depending on how much you charge, you can make that up your first or second month. Sound good so far? Let's get started.

Chapter I
Getting Started

<u>Business Structure</u>

Now one of the things you must think about first is what kind of business structure to set up. If you don't know what I'm talking about it that's ok. I didn't either at first. I can't tell you how to do this part because I'm not a lawyer or an accountant and it would be both illegal and unethical for me to do so. I can tell you the different types of business structures there are though at this writing. Consult with an attorney or an accountant about what would be best for you. Most of them will offer to set you up correctly and it doesn't cost a lot to do so. Some you can take care of yourself. We started out as a sole proprietorship because it was the simplest and easiest to do. Here are the structures I was talking about...

<u>SOLE PROPRIETORSHIP</u> – Easiest to do. One person owns the business. Taxes are filed quarterly and you file a 1040 at the end of the year as you've always done. However, I don't recommend doing your own taxes. Hire a CPA to do them.

<u>PARTNERSHIP</u> –A little more complicated. Both partners must file taxes. A little more costly. Not widely recommended. This one can cause problems if partners become adversaries.

<u>CORPORATION</u> – This one gets complicated. Shares are issued and the company can be publicly or privately held. Must register with your state of business. The person or group with the largest stock ownership makes the decisions. Records must be kept. There are two types of corporations- "S" and "C". A lot of paperwork !

LLC – (Limited Liability Company) – Kind of like a corporation only not as much to set up and a little less complicated.

There are others that I am not familiar with. I will suggest the following though because I learned the hard way. You may not want to consider forming a corporation until you really start making some money because tax time you will pay more in taxes and tax preparation costs!!

Business Name

This one is pretty self-explanatory. Think of a name that best describes your business. If it's going to be a mom and pop operation you might want a name that reflects that. Or if you want to go for more of a professional business feel, you will of course want a name that is more professional sounding. Just make sure the name isn't in use already.

Federal Tax ID Number

This you will need once you start actually doing business. You can download the form from the IRS website www.irs.gov or call your accountant to get the form.

Insurance

When starting out you will need to get bonding and liability insurance. Bonding insurance is pretty cheap and only costs around $100 per year. This protects your client against theft. Liability insurance is a little more but if you shop around you should be able to find relatively low rates also. This protects you should an accident occur or you have to replace a computer or something. Don't let this scare you off. Accidents rarely occur as long as you pay attention to what you're doing and if you hire good people you don't have to worry about thefts. This is like car insurance. You may not ever need it but it's good to have just in case. Don't worry about this until you have clients and are making money.

Phones

When starting out I suggest having a business cell phone line. Cell phone service is cheap and you can get voice mail for when you're not available. Since you are going to be out and about it would make sense to have a cell phone as your business phone so you don't miss any important phone calls. Shop around to find rates and services that will fit your needs. If you decide to go outside of town to do jobs you may want a cell phone that will reach farther out but not charge you much more.

You can buy a fax machine around $100-$150 and use your home phone for your fax line. (This is how we started out.) Or you can find a used one at a discount office furniture store.

Licenses & Permits

More that likely you will have to get a business license from your city or county that you operate in. These are relatively cheap. It costs us $20-30 per year to register our business with the city. Again, don't worry about this until your business is up and running. Focus on getting business for now!

Marketing

Here is the part I enjoy!! GETTING THE CUSTOMERS!! Look in the yellow pages. See all of those businesses? ALL OF THEM ARE POTENTIAL CLIENTS!!! The really good ones to go after are the Drs and dentists' offices as well as lawyers, accountants, etc. The ones that have the nice clean offices. Now I'm going to tell you the easiest and best way to get customers. These have been the best ways for us. In this business you have to go get the clients – they don't just come to you. At least not in the beginning. You have to prove yourself. Once you start cleaning and do a good job, the word will get out.

1) Direct Mail

Have some 5.5X3.5 post cards made up with return postage on them. Just provide a place to have them give some information and return them back to you. I've included a copy of one we use on the following page. You are welcome to copy from it and modify it to suit your needs. Any copying place can make these for you. A good online resource is www.vistaprint.com .You can put it in a 6.5 X 3 5/8 envelope and stamp it and they can mail it back to you or you can use the double sided ones where all they do is tear off the return part, fill it out and drop it in the mail. It costs a little more but it makes it easier for them. YOU WANT TO MAKE IT AS EASY AS POSSIBLE FOR YOUR PROSPECTS TO RESPOND TO YOUR MAILER! Do about 100 a month or however many you can afford. It only costs .57 per card to do. Or even less if you use the double-sided postcard. You should expect about a 2-3% return of mailers. That's actually about the norm for direct mail advertising. We've actually had a few of our first post cards come in from time to time wanting appointments. So that proves that these office managers hang on to these post cards and save them for later. Even if you get one or two accounts from every 100 cards, the responses will more than pay for it.

2) Cold Calling

This is actually getting out and pounding the pavement. Going from business to business and handing out your card. I had some brochures made up and handed them out. I actually ended up with a few accounts by doing this. Just make sure when you go into these businesses that you have something to hand to them. The brochures I had made cost about $80 for 100 of them and they last quite awhile. Again a good place to check for inexpensive printing is www.vistaprint.com Also have some business cards made up. We had 1000 made up for about $65. Or nowadays you can make them up on your computer at home with the right paper and program.

3) Referral or word of mouth

This will happen after you've been in business for a while. Tell your new customers that you are looking for new clients and that they are free to refer you around. Give them some kind of incentive like cleaning windows or maybe even some kind of cash bonus for referring you to a new customer. Only do this after you have the new account and they are paying promptly each month. If you do a good job the referrals will come your way!

www.cnscleaning.com

We Clean up after some of the finest professionals in Wichita.

Hi, we are Chad & Shannon Burns, owners of C & S Cleaning Service. We offer personalized office cleaning at reasonable rates. We also offer floor cleaning services.

If you feel you're not getting the service you deserve or want that personal touch, fill out this postage paid card. You can also call 992-6885 or 993-3245 for a convineat meeting.

Name: _____

Street: _____

City: _____ State: _____ Zip: _____

Phone: _____ Best time to Call: _____

4) <u>Local Business Phone Book</u> – If your area has it, get your hands on the local phone book most utilized by businesses and get a small ad in there to start out. We have always gotten calls from ours and have had an ad in it from the beginning. It legitimizes you as a business. When people need a new cleaning company –they go to the phone book...It's a fact.

5) <u>Networking</u>

Another good way to start getting clients is to network with other cleaning companies and join cleaning associations and going to seminars. This sounds odd but as a well known copywriter said "A rising tide lifts all boats". I agree with that. If everyone in the janitorial industry worked to improve the image of the industry – we would be able to demand bigger fees as well as would earn more respect from our clients. Plus if you team up with a larger firm, when they have too much work – they will call you to subcontract and take care of the work for them.

We currently partner with another cleaning company and it is working beautifully. We have become friends with the owners and we have lunch together at least once every couple of weeks so that we can catch up and see what we can do better. We throw each other work when we are too swamped to do it ourselves. We even collaborate when we need to hire new employees. Make sure when you subcontract for another company or even if it's just collaboration – take care of that relationship. If you do a poor job and hurt their business they will never call you again.

Networking can be very profitable for you. Find new ways to get out there and find clients. Join the local Chamber of Commerce. Go to business seminars, mixers, and luncheons. This is an excellent way to make new sales leads. If a business owner sees you at one of these functions it will automatically add credibility to your business. It will also show them you are serious about your business.

The gist about networking is – find new ways to get in front of business decision makers. It will pay off – maybe not right away but if you make a good impression, they will remember you later when they are ready to make a change.

How to do it

Now grab the yellow pages and GO FOR IT!! Good ones to start mailing to are accountants, Dentists, medical offices, optometrists, and lawyers. These all have nice clean offices that will be easy to clean and maintain.

A little secret for advertising – NEVER do advertising on Mondays or Fridays – Mondays are always too busy of a day to go cold calling and more than likely if they get your card on Monday it's going in the trash because they are too busy to look at it. Fridays everyone is thinking about the weekend and not wanting to start anything new. Focus on doing your mailings and marketing Tuesday through Thursday.

Always keep doing mailings as you can afford to. The reason behind this is you want to get the easiest accounts for the most money! Let's face it, there are only so many hours in the day and you want to maximize those hours to make the most money! Keep mailing and keep putting your name out there – it will get noticed! You might mail an office a card at a time when they are thinking of switching services. That's why you should always keep mailing!!

Also when you get the money, put a small ad in the local business phone book. I GUARANTEE you'll get calls from it. A carpet cleaning company we subcontract with has a FULL PAGE ad and they get 30-50 calls a month!

A word of advice about marketing

Listen, just because you hang out your shingle doesn't mean the customers will come beating down your door. This business, just like any business requires real work and REAL effort. If you just do a little bit every day or as you can afford to – IT WILL PAY OFF! The janitorial industry is one of the easiest to get into. Why? Because if it exists in the physical world – sooner or later it will need cleaned. But as with any business you have to let people know you are here. A businessman once said "You can have the greatest thingamajig in the world – but if no one knows about it, it won't matter."

That's why your first thing you should do is <u>get your customers</u>! Without them you have a business name – THAT'S IT! Most people don't have the first clue about starting a business so they go out and buy a bunch of office equipment and have some business cards made up. Pay a bunch of fees to get licenses, etc. and then they have no money to put into marketing to get clients. And they sit back and scratch their heads wondering where they went wrong.

"The customer is king" – remember that phrase and you will do fine. GO GET YOUR CUSTOMER FIRST BEFORE YOU DO ANYTHING ELSE!

Chapter II
Doing the Interview

Ok, now you got one of your mailers back and you've set the appointment. Now you want to be prepared when you go into the interview. So here are a few things to do.

1)   Dress professionally–You want to project an image of professionalism and also look like you know what you're doing. Remember – You can only make a first impression ONCE! Make it a GOOD one!!

2)   Have something to hand your new prospect – it can be a business card or even a brochure. I would hand a business card to them with a list of services that will be included in the cost of them having you clean for them.

3)   Make up a short questionnaire of things that you will want to ask them. Such as:

   a)   Have they had service before?
   b)   How many square feet is the area to be cleaned?
   c)   What did they like about their last service?
   d)   What did they not like about their last service?
   e)   What did they charge to clean for them?

These last three will give you ideas as to what they expect and want from you to clean for them. The last question is optional. They may tell you or they may not. If you think the interview is going well and you think they'll tell you go ahead and ask. It will give you a good idea as to what to charge for a building their size. If they ask, just tell them you want to make sure they aren't paying too much for service.

4)   Make sure and measure out the area to be cleaned. Don't just take their word for it. They may not be trying to intentionally mislead you but they could just be plain off in their estimate. You can get a rolling measuring tape at any hardware store or home improvement store. It will be easier to use than trying to use a plain old measuring tape.

5)   If they ask you for a quote right there just tell them you have to do some figuring and it will take a day or two to get one put together – Remember you need to figure in costs as well as taxes, etc and what you want to make off of the deal. Most everyone will allow a day or two for you to get back with them. Once you do a hundred or so bids you may be able to quote them right there. I still don't advise it though. I usually sit down and think about the routine, how long to clean, if I put an employee in there to clean it, etc. That's why it's good to sit down and go over everything before you give a price.

6)   Most places will supply toilet paper, paper towels, soap, trash bags, etc. Make sure you line out who will be supplying what so there is no misunderstanding. If they want you to supply everything – add at least 10-20% to your bid to cover your costs if you decide to supply everything. My suggestion is – try to get them to take care of it. That way you don't have to mess with ordering, stocking, etc.

7)   Thank them for their time and the opportunity to come talk to them. Make sure they know how and when you will be giving them your bid. Whether it's by fax, phone or written proposal –make sure you respond promptly! Don't leave them hanging and wondering when they will get your bid. When starting out it is preferable that you send them a written bid and spell out everything in it.

8)   Let them know that you are just starting out and you would love to be able to prove yourself to them. They will appreciate the honesty and will more than likely give you the chance. Once you start to get clients under your belt, put together a reference list that you can hand out. Until then, let your new prospects know that you are just getting started.

I have included a basic checklist of things that are pretty common and included in the monthly cost of office cleaning. You can use it as a basis and add or subtract from it as you see fit –it's your business!

I have also included a sample bid letter. Adjust to fit your needs.

The first time you clean any account will always take the longest. As you become more familiar with it you will get faster. This will allow you more time to do more jobs. Remember you can work as much or as little as you want. And you can hire people to do the work for you and you just go find the jobs, but we'll get into that later!!

Chapter III
Bidding and Pricing

Ok, now you've met with your new prospect, found out what they want, measured out the area and looked at what you will need for the job.

First off let me say that there is no hard and fast rule to bidding on a job. It's pretty much whatever will get you the account and still make you enough money to be worth the account. If the client is really dirty you should charge more as it will take you longer. If they aren't and would be pretty easy to do then don't price yourself out of range.

I don't know what the rates are around the country but here in the Midwest, the hourly rate for cleaning goes for around $25.00-$40.00 per hour. The rates for square footage goes for anywhere between .09 - .14 per square foot. A good way to find out what the local rates are is to call some of the cleaners who have been in business for a while and see what they are charging. Call them up and act like you are a business that is looking for cleaning service and see if they will tell you what their rates are and what they include etc.

Also as you get bigger and if you decide to take on employees you will need to figure in insurance, sales tax, and payroll tax into your bids so you don't short change yourself.

If you have Internet access there are a few sites that are good for bidding and good for information on the cleaning industry. I've included a few for you to use.

www.issa.com - Good resource site to use to find information, ask questions, etc.

www.BigMop.com - This site actually has a bidding calculator you can use to figure what you would charge to clean, do carpets, strip & wax floors, etc.

www.alturasolutions.com - Another good resource site to use for questions, etc.

www.cleanfax.com - This site deals mainly with cleaning carpet but still a good resource to use. Posts news articles on cleaning from around the country.

There are different factors involved that will affect your pricing. These include:

-Size and cleanliness of the building
-Services wanted. (If they want window cleaning, make that an extra charge.)
-How many times per week service is needed.
- I also include something I call my "Pain in the butt factor" - How much is this client going to be a pain the butt for me to keep clean. Some will be really picky. Others won't. You will get a feel for this when you do the interview. Just make sure you add a little something in for this.

Floor care services and window cleaning should be charged separately from office cleaning. (If you want to get into that area of the office cleaning business.)

Remember that whatever price gets you the job and still makes you your money is what you should bid. Just make sure to include ALL costs in on top of your profit – (Which is at least 20%). Don't be afraid to ask what they are paying now, tell them you are just starting out and would love to prove yourself. They may actually tell you! If they do, keep that in mind so you can make your figure around that. You should be able to underbid the current company starting out but don't bid so low as to reduce your hourly rate.

A word about bidding – You don't necessarily always want to be the lowest bid. Although a lot of companies base their decision on that, it's not always the deciding factor. It also depends on what you offer and the VALUE of your bid. You may provide everything that every other company provides but say you agree to do their windows once a month or something for free. THAT may get you the customer right there. Add value to your bids. It will make all the difference!

We currently use a combination of hourly and square footage to figure our bids. You may want to try several different ways to see what works best for you.

You may also want to give them several bids, such as one for basic services, one for basic services plus window cleaning, etc. This will give them a choice of which one to take. Plus if you give them more than one option, more than likely they will pick one instead of going somewhere else. People love having choices, so this may be the way for you to go. We've tried it a few times and it has worked well.

When starting out, buy your supplies from a discount store (Wal-Mart, Kmart) or from a big warehouse type place (Sam's Club) where you can buy in bulk. It will be cheaper if you do it that way. As you get bigger you can establish an account with a local janitorial supply house that will set you up with an account where you can order your supplies and equipment and then pay for them on a "Payable in 30 days" type set up. That way you can get your supplies, do the job, collect your money and THEN pay the invoice.

Buy your vacuum from a local store like Wal-Mart, Kmart or whatever. As you start to make more money you can get a commercial vacuum to use later. Some places will supply a vacuum but you should have one just in case.

We have recently found that backpack vacuums are time savers and you get in a lot more places with them than a conventional vacuum.

Keep in mind that all supplies you buy for the business are tax deductible as well as all equipment. When you get established you should sit down with your accountant to determine tax liability, etc.

YOUR FIRST ACCOUNT!!

Once your new client accepts your proposal, you will need to draw up an agreement or contract to spell out everything that you agree to do, how much your client pays a month, etc. There is a lot of good software out there for drawing up simple contracts you can use or simply use your own computer to draw one up yourself using a word processing program such as Microsoft Word or WordPad. Just make sure you have a written agreement between yourself and your new client. It will prevent headaches later on and will make sure both parties know what is expected in the monthly service and what will be extra charges.

Sometimes you will find once you get going in an account, a client will want more or different services. Agree on a price and then go ahead and do them. Just make sure you have something in writing. Having them sign a new agreement is the best thing. I know all of this sounds like a headache but it will save you in the end.

A good clause to throw in your contract is that your client accepts the terms of the contract and understands that anything not specifically written out will be an extra charge. It will keep clients from wanting you to do a bunch of little extras that some of them will try to get you to do without having to pay for them. Let them know up front that this is your business and anything extra is going to be an extra charge! You don't stay in business by doing things for free and in this business, TIME IS MONEY!

Make sure you include payment terms and if they are late they agree to pay late charges, etc. You want to let them know you are serious about getting paid. You can't live off of good intentions.

In writing up the length of the contract, I wouldn't make it for longer than 6 mos at a time. If things go bad or management changes hands and they want to bring someone else in you don't want to be somewhere you're not wanted. Even if you're doing a good job and want to stay. It might be a good idea to throw another clause in your contracts stating that if both parties agree, you can dissolve the contract at anytime. It may save you some headache later on.

BigMop.com used to have a good sample contract you can use as a guideline. If not, there are all sorts of cheap and free software on the Internet that you can get to make up simple contracts. They usually are no more than $5. You can go to myfreesoftware.com ! They have all sorts of free and cheap software you can get for your business. Just make sure you get something in writing! It's just good business anymore. I'm sure there are people you could do business on their word, but in today's business world you have to protect yourself.

A word about customers

Sometimes you will find that no matter what you do –your customer is not happy. You have cleaned the place so that it shines on a cloudy day and they are still complaining. At this point you have two options.

1)   Give your notice and get out of the agreement.
2)   Work the account until THEY give their 30 day notice.

I usually opt for the second one. That way the money keeps rolling in as long as possible. Remember this is a business deal. Just because you can't make them happy doesn't mean you aren't doing a good job. There are people in this world that you just can't make happy. You should do everything in your power to make your customer happy but don't do it to where you are doing things outside of your agreement.

I have a little saying "The customer is always right – TO A POINT!" And when that point comes, it's time to part company. You should bend over backwards to keep a customer but don't let them push you around. You are a business owner and if they don't value what you do for them – you don't want them for a customer. There are plenty more out there to get that will appreciate what you do for them. I have some of those customers and I bend over backwards for them. It pays off in the form of extra work and they happily pay the extra fees that I charge them because I do such a good job on their everyday cleaning.

You don't need or want headache customers. There are too many good ones out there for you to be fooling with problems. And they are a lot more profitable!

I will leave it up to you but if you can stand it – stick it out until they give you notice but keep up your best work even after they give you their notice. It's best to part company on good terms and keep the check coming in as long as possible.

Chapter IV
Expanding Your Business

The good thing about this business is you can EASILY make a full time living working part time or you can expand, take on employees and REALLY make a nice living!!

My wife and I have been in business for 6 years at this writing and currently have 5 employees and are doing over $100,000 in business a year! And we only work ourselves 5-6 hours a night. We have built a new house, have an RV and two newer cars. As you can see this is truly a safe business to get into as this business keeps going no matter what the economy is doing! Everyone needs cleaning and no one wants to do it themselves so they have to PAY someone else to do it!

There are so many ways to expand in this business that I can't even list them all. But here are a few ways to expand and make even MORE money on top of just office cleaning.

Floor cleaning

This is a very common and very lucrative area to get into. Even if you don't know how to strip & wax floors most local janitorial supply houses have books and even hold classes on how to clean and wax floors. The machines cost some money but as you're starting out you can rent or lease them from the supply houses until you start getting enough work to justify buying a machine.

Carpet Cleaning

Again a very good area to get into. Especially in residential carpet cleaning. There are a limitless # of houses to do. I suggest taking classes to learn this though as to learn spot removal, different types of carpet cleaning, etc. This is a little more complicated than doing strip & waxing floors, as there are different types of carpets and different ways to clean carpets.

Window Cleaning

This is a good extra to add to your cleaning services and an area that is overlooked a lot! I know some people that charge as much as 5$ per window. Again it's whatever makes it worth your while as well as makes the client happy.

Mini Blind Cleaning

This is still a virtually untapped market! There is more work in this area than I can name. Some good methods of cleaning mini-blinds can be found on the Internet and on eBay©. If you would like more information on this email me (cburns31@cox.net). We currently don't do this type of cleaning yet but I haven't ruled it out. There is just too much potential here!

Hiring Employees

If you get so busy that you need to hire help, my best suggestion is to rent a place to hold interviews, such as a hotel conference room and place an ad in your local paper giving instructions on the time, place of interview and what the starting pay is so as to eliminate 1,000 phone calls and the so called "lookers". (People who don't really need or want a job but are looking for something else.) Remember to ask detailed questions such as why they want the job and what they are looking for. Check references and conduct background checks in both criminal and how many times they have claimed workers' compensation. Background checks only cost about $30 per person so be serious about the person you are hiring before you spend money for a background check. You don't want to hire someone who is going to work a week and claim an injury and put you out of business.

A good place to find employees is from your clients. Most of them will have a co-worker with a son or daughter who needs a part time job or also retired people are a good source for employees. They do a good job and are dependable because they need something to take up some extra time but they can only make so much due to the restrictions the government puts on retirees' income. Check with local churches and retirement homes to find these people.

Another good way we have found is to advertise for help on the internet. This way you know they are half way intelligent and you will find a better class of employee. I don't mean to belittle anyone but I can tell you some horror stories about employees just because I didn't know any better. Usually your local paper will have some kind of ad setup on the internet that you can advertise in the help wanted section.

One thing I will advise against is hiring friends and family. Most times they think they can do whatever and they will expect a bigger check because they are friend or family. They think because they are family- they should have a stake in the business and make what you make. As the saying goes – "Don't go there!"

As you get going you will need to take on additional insurance such as workers compensation insurance. Shop around for a good provider and rates so you can afford to stay in business and keep making money.

Check into local resources offered by the government and local colleges. Most of them will have SBA sponsored programs such as SCORE (Service Corps Of Retired Executives) and SBDCS. (Small Business Development Centers) that offers free advice and resources to small businesses starting up or already in business. You can go to them at any time for help and they are an invaluable resource as these are people who have already been in business and have been down the road you are going now! They also hold seminars on different aspects of running a business on an ongoing basis for a nominal fee. Check into this, as it will be a BIG help to you in getting your business up and running.

SAMPLE LIST

C & S Cleaning Service

---

www.cnscleaning.com

Services Offered

- Empty Wastebaskets: Change liners as needed
- Empty and damp clean ashtrays
- Dust & Damp clean desks (if desired), chairs, tables, shelves, cabinets and any horizontal surfaces.
- Vacuum carpeted areas
- Clean entryway doors & glass
- Dust blinds
- Dust for cobwebs, etc.
- Spot clean walls, doors, partitions for prints
- Spot clean carpet (excludes steam cleaning – Min. charge $25per 250 sq. ft.)
- Clean mirrors, countertops, etc.
- Replace paper goods as needed
- Sanitize and damp mop floors
- Clean & sanitize sinks, toilet bowls, etc.

*Services also available

- Specialized floor care available!!
- Carpet Cleaning available! (Hot water extraction)
- Window Cleaning available!!

(* Can be included in a package deal negotiated on site- by- site basis)

If you don't see what you need – please ask your representative!

SAMPLE BID LETTER

C & S Cleaning Inc.
www.cnscleaning.com
BID # 3-2102

March 21, 2002

RE: Bid

Tina
ABC Realty and Investments, Inc.
1234 S Washington
Wichita, Ks 67211

Dear Tina,

Thank you for considering our cleaning service
After looking over your facilities at 1234 S Washington, I propose a bid of $585.00 for monthly janitorial service. This bid includes service 3 times a week including window cleaning once a week. This bid covers all supplies, labor, equipment and all applicable taxes.
Services include:
Vacuum all carpeted areas
Empty all trash & reline containers
Clean & Sanitize Bathrooms
Restock paper goods
Sweep & damp mop all tile floor
High & low dust as needed
Clean windows once a week

Carpet care and floor services are available for a separate fee if desired.

This bid is valid for 10 business days and is subject to change.

References and proof of insurance available upon request.

Please feel free to contact me should you have any questions.

Sincerely
Chad Burns –President
C & S Cleaning Inc

CONCLUSION

This business is one that has been around for a long time and will be around for even longer!! Everything needs cleaned sooner or later and someone somewhere will pay someone to clean it for them. If you were to find a specialty type of cleaning and focus on it you would probably make a small fortune!! EVERYTHING NEEDS CLEANED AT SOME TIME!!!

That's the great thing about this business! There is NO LIMIT to what you can do with it! In five years I can hardly believe how far we've come and we have barely even gotten started! I can't wait to see where we are after ten years!

This business can work in ANY type of economy. Whether in a recession or a booming one! It works especially well in a booming one because businesses want extra services which means extra $$$$!!

Realistically you CAN make $40,000 part-time. We currently service 12 clients at an average of $708.00 per client per month. If you had only 5 per month at that amount (708 X 5 = $3540) ($3540 X 12 = 42480). So you see it IS possible!!

Another great thing is you can start this business ANYWHERE!!! Everyone everywhere needs cleaning! This is definitely a business that will always be in demand!!

I wish you all good luck and good fortune! I hope I have provided you with all of the information you need to do this business. If not, feel free to email me at cburns31@cox.net and I will do my best to answer all of your questions. I am not providing my business # as I am too busy to answer the phone all day and answer questions but I do respond to my email on a regular basis so feel free to contact me that way.

Just remember to get out there and get your customer first. And do a good job! Your work says a lot about you. And you want to put your best foot forward. I wish you all the best!

To your success!

Chad Burns

Questions and Answers

---

1.   How do I get started in this business?

First think of a business name, make up some business cards, use the postcard I've provided to make up some mailers and start mailing to EVERY business in the yellow pages!

2.   Do I need to worry about insurance and licenses and stuff now?

No, worry about getting business right now. After you get rolling and get some money coming in, then check into getting insurance, required permits & licenses etc.

3.   Where do I buy my cleaning supplies at?

Buy them in bulk at a local discount store such as Sam's Club or Wal-Mart or somewhere like that. It will be cheaper starting out and you can set up an account at a janitorial supply house later.

4.   What do I do when I get a client to respond to a postcard?

Call them back and set an appointment. Dress professionally and take them a business card or brochure. Look over the business and measure out the area to be cleaned. Thank them for their time and then go home and figure out what it would take to clean it and still make you some money. Respond promptly with an offer.

5.   What do I do if I get a client who won't pay?

DROP THEM RIGHT AWAY!! You can't get rich off of clients who won't pay and you will run across them from time to time. It's just part of business. Don't waste your time taking them to court. You can't get blood out of a turnip!

6.   Should I hire employees right away or just do the jobs myself?

Starting out I would do the jobs myself. Once you become established, then you can start hiring employees. BUT GO SLOW!! Don't get in over your head. Also if you do plan to make it a full time business, talk to your accountant about tax liability, money to expand, etc. TAKE IT SLOW!! You can make it what you want to make it.

7.   What kind of money can I make in this business?

Realistically you can make anywhere between 30,000-50,000 working part time. Full time-THE SKY'S THE LIMIT!!

8.   What kind of taxes will I have to pay as a business owner?

Everyone has to pay income tax. As far as the others, consult with your accountant as tax law varies from state to state. Find this out before you get a phone call or letter from the IRS!!

9.   What if a client wants a service I don't provide like carpet cleaning?

First off don't panic. If you can't provide the service yourself, let them know that up front. Tell them you'd be happy to refer them or you can tell them that you would love the chance to do it yourself if they are willing. Just be sure to consult with someone who's in the business BEFORE you try to do the job yourself. You can usually get help on different cleaning topics at your local janitorial supply house and it's usually free!

10.   Can I sell the business when I'm ready to get out of it?

Absolutely!! This is a legitimate business that you can sell yourself in the Business Opportunity section of the Classified Ad section of the newspaper. Or if you have the time and money you can have a business broker assess it and sell everything (equipment,etc.) for a nice chunk of cash!! Established businesses usually sell pretty quickly. Especially a business like this because it is a cash business.

Summary

1.   You will need to decide on how to set up your business and choose a name for it. Consult with an attorney or accountant on this matter.

2.   Once you start to get clients you will need to apply for a Federal ID #. This form is available on the internet at www.irs.gov or consult with your accountant. You will also need bonding and liability insurance. Don't worry about these until after you get some clients and some money rolling in.

3.   You will also need to get a business license and register your business locally. This will also give you credibility with your prospects. Again don't worry about this until after you have some clients.

4.   Use a cellular phone as your business line at first. The services these days are relatively inexpensive and you can use voicemail as an answering service. You don't want to miss an important sales call because you are cleaning. Also you don't want to pay to put another phone line in and have your home phone ringing at all hours of the day. Buy a simple fax machine and hook it up to your home phone to use as your fax #.

5.   The best way to get clients is to use a return postage paid postcard. Make it as simple as possible for your prospects to respond. Your yellow pages is your target market. ALWAYS KEEP MAILING!! You want to get the easiest and best paying clients and keep them! You can use the sample I provided to make up your cards. This is proven and it works!!!

6.   You can also get some brochures made up and get out and pound the pavement to get customers. Also if you do a good job, the referrals will start to roll in.

7.   Once you get a card back and set the appointment, dress professionally and take something to hand to your prospect whether it's a business card or brochure.

8.   Ask questions about what they want and don't want so you don't repeat the same mistakes as the last cleaning service. Try to get them to supply all paper goods & soap so you don't have to fool with ordering & stocking supplies.

9.   Make sure and measure out the area and take a good look at what's going to be needed.

10.   Thank them for their time and be sure and follow up with your bid promptly.

11.   If you're just starting out, tell them you'd love to prove yourself. They may appreciate the honesty and give you a job right there.

12.   When you bid a job, make sure you include all costs, including labor, all taxes and supplies needed as well as the profit you wish to make. There is no hard and fast rule to bidding a job. It's whatever gets you the job and makes you enough to make it worth while. There are sites on the Internet I have included to help you as well as tips to finding out pricing in your area. Bidding a job depends on different factors. Make sure to include them all.

13.   Buy your cleaning supplies in bulk from a discount store. It will be cheaper for you starting out. You can set up an account with a janitorial supply house as you grow.

14.   You can make this business as big or as small as you want. You can do carpet cleaning, floor cleaning, window cleaning and even branch out into house cleaning if you want! It's all up to you! If you want to just do this on the side for vacation money or for a new car –YOU CAN!! Or you can hire employees, buy equipment and make it a full time business and really make some BIG MONEY!!! That's what's so great about this business. You can make it what you want to make it. SO:

15.   Think of a business name, make up some postcards and business cards and GO FOR IT!!! You'll be glad you did!

www.ingramcontent.com/pod-product-compliance
Lightning Source LLC
Chambersburg PA
CBHW051258170526
45165CB00004B/1768